Neymar: A Boy Who Became A Star.

ISBN-13: 978-1-948040-04-4
ISBN-10: 1-948040-04-2

First Edition: December 2017
10 9 8 7 6 5 4 3 2 1

Neymar grew up in a poor family in Brazil.

Neymar's father was a former soccer player.

His father inspired him to never give up on his dream.

Neymar loved to play soccer as a kid. His father always encouraged him to keep improving his skills, and helped Neymar became an all-star he is today.

Some people think Neymar was just lucky.
But it's not true.
In order to win, Neymar must always practice.
Talent doesn't come to those who sit around.

Every day, he would practice - with friends, by himself, at home, or outside.

If there was any chance he could get to improve his skills, he took it and gave it his best.

The excitement of chasing the ball, and the joy of scoring the goals were the reasons Neymar loved soccer so much.

At the age of 14, Neymar traveled to Spain and joined the Real Madrid young team, and he got to play with other amazing players.

Barcelona is one of the best soccer clubs in the world.

Together with Lionel Messi and Luis Suarez, Neymar had created the best attacking trio for Barcelona.

They were the most powerful attacking trio in Spanish soccer history.

They were unstoppable and scored the most goals of the season.

After so many success with Barcelona, Neymar moved to another club in France called Paris Saint-German.
He became the most valuable soccer player in the world.

Neymar is unstoppable, and he is on his quest to become one of the best soccer players of all time.

Neymar has his dad who helped him to become the great soccer player he is today.

Chances are, you have someone in your life who wants you to succeed, too. Listen to them, keep practicing and you will be successful one day!

Thank you for reading my story!
Did you like the book?
If you like it, please write a review on Amazon. Tell me what you think!
I look forward to reading your review!

Made in the USA
Las Vegas, NV
10 March 2024

86968466R00024